# MLK & LI
## Martin Luther King, Jr. and Long Island

by Allison Singh
Illustrated by
Sergio Garzon

© 2021 Allison Singh
New York
www.ithappenedonli.com
ISBN 978-1-7353395-2-8

Every Martin Luther King, Jr. Day
students learn about places in the South
like Greensboro, Selma and
Montgomery, where important battles of
the Civil Rights Movement took place.

**Greensboro, North Carolina**

1

These places can seem very
far away.

Selma, Alabama

Montgomery, Alabama

You may not know
that the Civil
Rights Movement
was fought all
over the United
States—probably
right in your
home town!

2

This is true for Long Island.

On Martin Luther King, Jr. Day it is important
to remember King's visits to Long Island,
and why he came.

Martin Luther King, Jr.'s first trip to Long Island was in
December 1962. The Long Island Committee for
Human Rights invited King to speak
at the Garden City Hotel.

King was the face of the Civil Rights Movement at the
time.  His visit sent the message that the battle for
equality in education, housing and employment was
being fought on Long Island.  This battle was
about to reach a new level.

The year 1963 was unlike any other for Long Island
students.  When the state instructed local school
districts to adopt integration plans,
many Long Island towns resisted.


Blacks on Long Island knew they would have
to fight  for equality in education.


They were not new to this fight.


They were ready.

After the Civil War, some Long Island towns built schools
for black children, but they were not given the same resources
as white schools.
In 1895, black Amityville resident and Civil War veteran
Charles D. Brewster tried to enroll his son in the town's
newer and better
funded white school.

The town said no.

**New Amityville school built for white students, 1895**
**Amityville Historical Society**

Brewster and other families boycotted the black
school and organized an economic protest.

The state agreed with Brewster.
The black school was closed.
Children of all races were educated together.

Brewster's actions inspired parents to demand
equal education for their children.

In 1900, New York Governor Teddy Roosevelt
outlawed segregated black schools.  This led to the
closure of all-black schools in Long Island towns
such as Hempstead, Jamaica and Flushing.

The last black school to close in New York State was
located on Long Island, in Roslyn.

It closed in 1917.

So what happened between
1917 and 1963?

Schools were not segregated by law,
but they were still segregated
because people from different
races were not living in
the same neighborhoods.
Most students on Long Island
attended the school closest to their
home.  As long as neighborhoods
were segregated,
schools would be, too.

That was the challenge facing
Long Island in 1963.

8

New York saw an answer in the Princeton Plan.

In Princeton, New Jersey, students were grouped
into elementary schools by grade level, not
neighborhood.  Under the Princeton Plan, students
of all races in the same grade attend school together.
The schools would be integrated, not segregated.
New York officials sought to bring this
plan to Long Island schools.

When Long Island school districts refused to comply
with the state's integration order, parents and
community groups fought back.  They held marches,
boycotts, sit-ins, pickets and even hunger strikes.
Mothers of black students were arrested when they
tried to register their children in the white schools.

**Students protesting at the Woodfield School in Malverne**

King visited Long Island during these school
integration battles.  In May of 1965 King held rallies in
Hempstead, Inwood, Long Beach, Lakeview
and West Hempstead.  With him was John Lewis and
other leaders in the Civil Rights Movement.

## KING SCORES SENATE AT RALLY IN NASSAU

Special to The New York Times

WEST HEMPSTEAD. L. I., May 12—The Senate's rejection of a ban on poll taxes in state elections was called "tragic" tonight by the Rev. Dr. Martin Luther King Jr.

Addressing 5,000 persons at a rally in the Island Garden Arena, Dr. King said that the "system of segregation is on its death bed and the only question now is how costly the segregationists will make the funeral."

The rally was sponsored by the Long Island Committee for the Southern Christian Leadership Conference. Other speakers were Senator Jacob K. Javits, Republican of New York, and John Lewis. national director of the Student Nonviolent Coordinating Committee.

**The New York Times, May 13, 1965**

## King's LI Tour Brings Throngs To the Streets

By Thomas A. Johnson

Twenty Negro men rushed up the stairs of a Long Island boarding house, stepped gingerly onto the roof, and began to cheer lustily—echoing the roar that came from 25 others on a roof across the road, and the estimated 800 more massed in the narrow street below.

**Newsday, May 13, 1965**

It took several years, but by 1966 most of the
schools did adopt plans to
end school segregation.

King speaking at rally in Long Beach with LI CORE leader
Lincoln Lynch, May 12, 1965.

But there was still resistance.

After the Malverne school board voted to accept
an integration plan, a cross was burned on the
high school lawn.  This was a symbol used in the
South to intimidate blacks.

King connected the Civil Rights Movements in the North and South in his famous 1963 "I Have a Dream" speech at the March on Washington.  Do you know what he said about New York in that famous speech? He said:

"We cannot be satisfied as long as the Negro in Mississippi cannot vote and the Negro in New York believes he has nothing for which to vote."

**King speaking at the March on Washington for Jobs and Freedom, August 28, 1963.**

14

After the school integration battles, many white
students left the newly integrated schools, taking
tax revenue and political power with them.
Realtors, banks and insurance companies
all played a role in keeping
neighborhoods segregated.

Realtors did not take black families to see homes for sale in
white neighborhoods. Civil rights groups exposed this by
sending two families, one white and
one black, to the same realtor.
They got very different results based on their skin color.

"Block busting" was also common at this time. Investors
scared whites to sell their homes at a low price.  The same
investors then resold these homes to blacks at a higher
price, making a profit and locking in segregated housing
on Long Island for years to come.

Housing segregation was not new to Long Islanders.

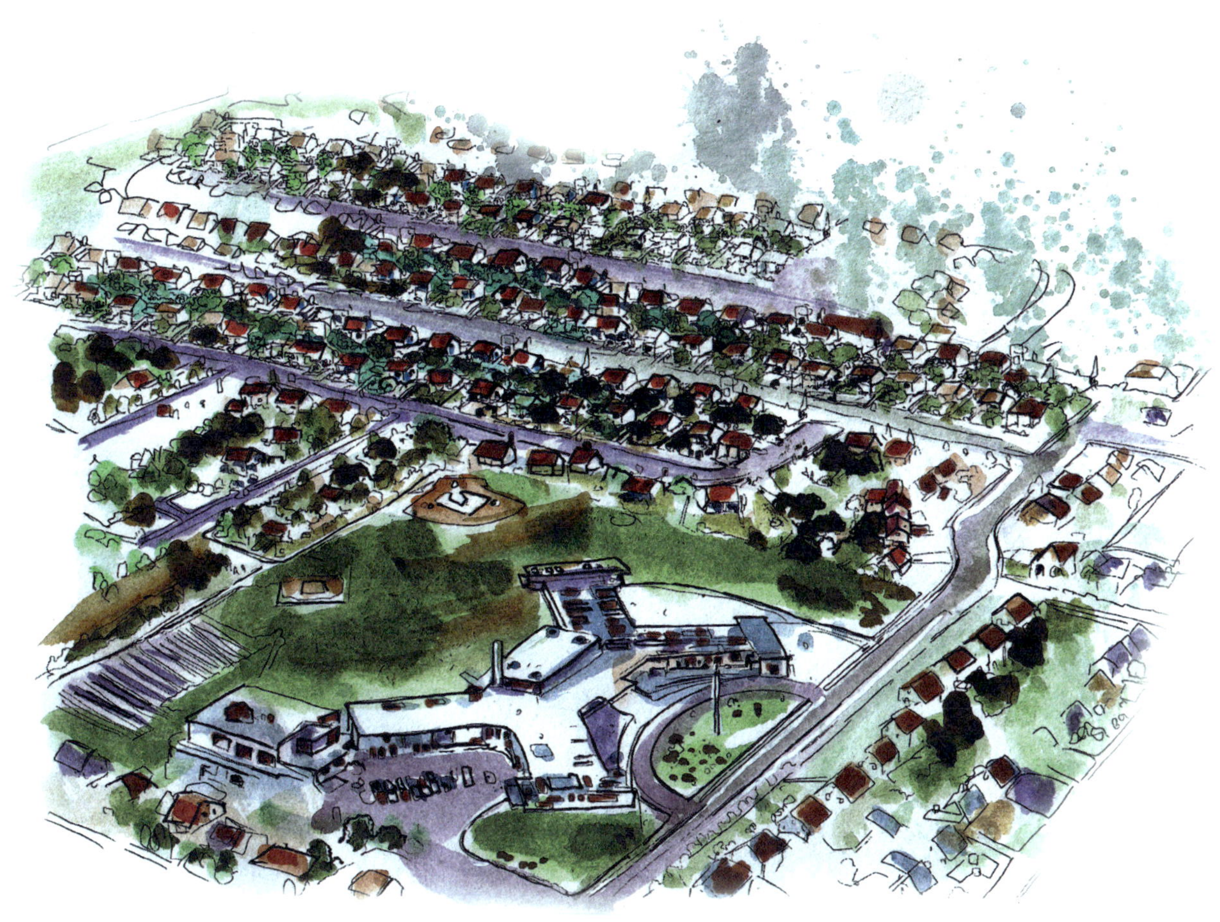

**Aerial view of post-WWII Levittown, Long Island**

After World War II, the company Levitt & Sons built thousands of inexpensive homes for soldiers returning home.  This part of Long Island is known as Levittown. Levitt & Sons refused to sell to blacks, or allow white buyers resell to blacks. The "American Dream" for sale in Levittown was denied to blacks.

King came to Queens College to speak in May 1965.
This was one year after Freedom Summer, when many
northern college students traveled to Mississippi to help
blacks register to vote.  Long Islander and Queens
College student Andrew Goodman was part of the
Freedom Summer movement. The Ku Klux Klan
murdered Goodman and two fellow volunteers
one day after he arrived in Mississippi.

King honored Goodman's legacy in his speech at
Queens College, saying he paid "the ultimate price" for
the struggle for civil rights,
but his death "was not in vain."

**Federal Bureau of Investigations (FBI)**

King also spoke these famous words that day in
Queens:

"Hate destroys the hater as well
as the hated."

One month later, King was back on Long Island.

In June 13, 1965, King spoke at the Hofstra
University graduation ceremony in Hempstead.
He called upon white people in the North to join
him in the fight for civil rights in their own
neighborhoods.  These were his words:

"It is just as important for the
white person in the North
to rise up with righteous indignation
when a Negro cannot
live in your neighborhood or
when a Negro cannot get a job
at your particular firm . . ."

King receiving an honorary doctorate from
Hofstra University President Clifford Lord

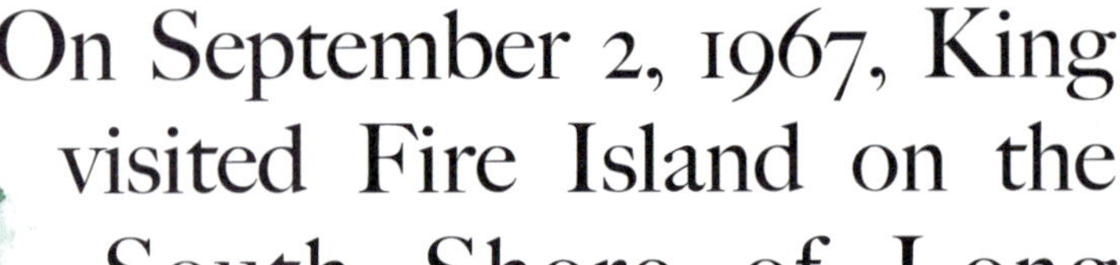

On September 2, 1967, King visited Fire Island on the South Shore of Long Island. He was invited to Seaview to give a speech and attend a fundraiser for the Civil Rights Movement. King was met by admiring crowds when he took the ferry to the island. Cars are not allowed on Fire Island. So upon reaching the island, King borrowed a bike and went for a ride.

Long Islanders hosted many fundraisers for King
like the one on Fire Island.  The two most successful
fundraisers for the Civil Rights Movement
in all of the United States were
held on Long Island,
in Great Neck and Garden City.

Why did the Civil Rights Movement need money?
One reason was to pay bail for the release of
protesters from jail.
Another was the cost of lawsuits challenging
segregation. Funds were also needed
for newspaper advertisements and rallies.

On March 26, 1968, King visited South Side Middle
School in Rockville Centre.  King spoke about racial
equality, the war in Vietnam and the new Poor People's
Campaign.  At the end, the mixed race crowd burst
into a standing ovation.  The Long Island Herald
newspaper wrote that King's message was
"needed on Long Island at the time."

**King speaking in the auditorium at South Side Middle School,
Rockville Centre.**

That was King's last trip to Long Island.

Nine days later, he was dead.

Long Islanders responded to King's assassination
with shock and action.

Students demanded a national holiday, a fight that would not be
won until 1983. Hofstra University offered full scholarships to
King's children. Levitt & Sons finally pledged to end
racial segregation in its building projects.
Long Island streets were renamed to honor King's legacy, and
Long Island towns celebrated King's birthday long before it
became a federal holiday.

As you can see, Martin Luther King, Jr. Day is not just about King's time in the South.

A coalition of many groups fought for civil rights on Long Island.  The National Association for the Advancement of Colored People (NAACP), the Congress of Racial Equality (CORE), churches and synagogues were joined by community groups such as the Great Neck Committee for Human Rights.

One of King's most famous writings is a letter
he wrote in June 1963 from a jail cell in
Birmingham, Alabama. In his "Letter from a
Birmingham Jail," King wrote:

"Injustice anywhere is a threat to justice
everywhere."

It is hard to learn that "injustice anywhere" is close to home, in the places we know and love.

But we can only have "justice everywhere" if we understand and act against the injustices right here at home.

# Learn More

## Books

Day, Lynda, R.  Making a Way to Freedom: A History of African Americans on Long Island.  New York: Empire State Books, 1997.

Mabee, Carleton.  Black Education in New York State.  New York: Syracuse University Press, 1979.

Verga, Christopher.  Civil Rights on Long Island.  New York: Arcadia Publishing, 2016.

## Articles

Howlett, Charles, F. "The Long Island Civil Rights Movement in the 1960s, Part One: The Struggle to Integrate Public Schools." The Long Island Historical Journal, Vol. 8, No. 2 (Spring 1996).

Winslow, Olivia.  "Long Island Divided, Part 10: Dividing Lines, Visible and Invisible — Segregation of Blacks, Whites Built into the History of Long Island." Newsday, November 17, 2019.

## Films

Defining Moments: The Civil Rights Movement in North Hempstead. https://www.mynhtv.com/civilrights

Dr. Martin Luther King, Jr. at Hofstra University (includes video of speech).  https://www.hofstra.edu/home/news/ur/ur_mlk.html

Oral Histories of the Civil Rights Movement on Long Island. https://www.mynhtv.com/civilrights

For many more resources, please visit
ithappenedonli.com/learnmore.

## About the Author

Allison Singh is a writer and lawyer from Long Island, New York.  She is the creator of the It Happened on LI series of picture books about lesser-known stories from Long Island history.  You can learn more about these books at: www.ithappenedonli.com


## About the Illustrator

Artist Sergio Garzon was born in Bogota, Colombia and lives and works in Honolulu, Hawai'i. As a professional illustrator, Garzon has been featured on NPR's "All Things Considered," Honolulu Star Advertiser and television networks covering his street art. He has 15 years of experience in hand-drawn design and illustration.

Made in the USA
Monee, IL
07 July 2026

56550198R00024